C000128400

IMAGES

*of America*

# MEADVILLE

Usually dated 1805, this map is a compilation of the 1792 David Mead survey and the 1795 resurvey by Maj. Roger Alden, Dr. Thomas Kennedy, and David Mead with additions of later land sales. It was copied in 1879 by J.F. Flagg, CCE, who appended detailed notes on the information sources and the methods he used in confirming their accuracy. The original map, which he worked from, was in the possession of William Reynolds and had been part of the estate of John Reynolds.

*On the cover*: Lloyd Singley greets his guests at a 1922 summer ice-cream social given for employees of the Keystone View Company. Like other contemporary firms of the period in Meadville, the Keystone View's labor policies were personal and paternalistic, and employees tended to stay for their whole careers.

IMAGES
*of America*

# MEADVILLE

Anne W. Stewart and William B. Moore

ARCADIA
PUBLISHING

Copyright © 2001 by Anne W. Stewart and William B. Moore
ISBN 978-1-5316-0582-7

Published by Arcadia Publishing
Charleston, South Carolina


Library of Congress Catalog Card Number: 2001091703

For all general information contact Arcadia Publishing at:
Telephone 843-853-2070
Fax 843-853-0044
E-mail sales@arcadiapublishing.com
For customer service and orders:
Toll-Free 1-888-313-2665

Visit us on the Internet at www.arcadiapublishing.com

At Bemustown, a low dam deflected water from French Creek into the French Creek Feeder
Canal to supply water to the Beaver & Lake Erie Canal, the westernmost arm of the Pennsylvania
Canal system. The feeder traveled south through Meadville to Shaw's Landing aqueduct, then
northwest to Conneaut Lake and Summit, a total of 27 miles. There, its waters were pumped
by steam engine to lock boats over the Lake Erie and Allegheny River Basins divide. Sartorius,
a prolific local artist, shows here the lock, dam, and mule corral still in place 20 years after the
canal had been closed to commercial use. In a touch of whimsy, he features the lock keeper's
dog and a fisherman reeling in a hellbender, an oversized, 29-inch-long unique salamander of
the French Creek watershed.

# CONTENTS

Today, this is Diamond Park. In the first half of the 19th century, it was a dusty militia drill grounds and a drover's corral. Following the Civil War, it became the public square with trees, grass, statues, and monuments. In the 20th century, it solidified its role as the heart of the city's institutional district, surrounded by churches, schools, an armory, a library, the courthouse, law offices, and mansions. Scene of Memorial Day observances, art shows and craft fairs, children's days and holiday celebrations, this green island is the city's central park. It is seen here in a 1953 aerial view by photographer Reed McCaskey.

# INTRODUCTION

Northwestern Pennsylvania has sometimes seemed to be history's stepchild, albeit a rich one. Claimed but only lightly settled by the Iroquois Confederacy, it was nominally under Seneca control. English royal grants, based on civilian settlement, had given Pennsylvania's northern tier to Connecticut in its charter's "to the Southern sea" clause. Uncertain of or careless of the geography of its American possessions, the crown gave to Virginia some of the same land in the drainage basin of the Allegheny River as part of its Ohio River rights.

Pennsylvania itself was initially limited to the area east of the Appalachians, and the crown attempted to keep peace with the Indian nations by forbidding trans-Appalachian settlement by the Proclamation Line of the 1763 Treaty of Paris, but Penn's heirs and the Colonial courts and legislature moved inexorably westward, beginning with the infamous walking treaty imposed on the Delawares.

The French throne was equally interested in these western lands. French missionaries and explorers had entered the American continent through the St. Lawrence and laid claim by discovery to most of the Great Lakes and Mississippi drainage basins. Traders and survey parties from Quebec, deLery in 1739 and Celeron in 1749, mapped and marked the area for the French king as the Iroquois watched (and likely later dug up) lead plates being placed by Celeron's troops.

As the atmosphere between Quebec and the English colonies heated up, the French began building forts throughout the huge watershed they required to maintain communication and supply between the French crown's northern Quebec area and its southern Louisiana lands. At the same time the Virginia colony, its soils depleted by tobacco cultivation, moved westward into its Ohio River claims. For the English colonies, American immigration had brought heavy demands for land. For the French, the crown sought the wealth of furs and trading to support its continental pretensions. Caught in the European struggle, the Iroquois negotiated to maintain space for their democratic confederacy, and the Delaware and other Algonquian seaboard nations, resisting whenever they were able, were forced into Canada or west as dependents into the territories of Plains and Prairie Nations.

Into this cauldron stepped a very young George Washington. A younger son, with minimal land holdings, seeking status in a class conscious society, Washington accepted the risky embassy of carrying a demand from Virginia's governor Robert Dinwiddie to Jacques LeGardeur de St Pierre, the new French commandant of the Venango River (French Creek) forts: France must remove its presence from the Ohio River basin. Accompanied by four major spokesmen for the Iroquois Confederacy—the half king Tanacharissen, the elder spokesman Juskaka, the orator White Thunder, and the hunter Guyasutha—and by seven Ohio Company traders and interpreters—John Davidson, Christopher G(e)ist, Jacob Van Braam, Barnaby Currin, John McGuire, Henry Steward, and William Jenkins—Washington made the 1753–1754 winter trip.

The embassy came to an eminently predictable conclusion (the French were not leaving), and the Virginians returned to their home bases. The French and Indian War ensued, neither France nor England being able to afford it or to afford avoiding it. Perhaps, in the long view, the most potent American result of Washington's embassy was the journal that he kept, which was widely published in the colonies and in England. In it, Washington recorded the rich bottom land, plentiful water, and first-growth forests through which he traveled. The French and Indian War and the American Revolution were to intervene, but the promise of those descriptions remained in men's minds and dreams.

Thirty-five years, in 1788, the Revolution over and the new U.S. Constitution adopted, David Mead and nine settlers set out for those fertile meadows. A Pennsylvania court had awarded him western lands to settle an earlier land dispute, and he knew just where he would find them. Following the Indian paths from Sunbury to the Allegheny River, taking the Venango Path to the confluence of French and Cussewago Creeks, he found the fertile soil, the plentiful clear streams, and the hardwoods and evergreens he needed to build a new community.

True, it was nearly 50 water miles from Franklin, the nearest American fort; it was 100 land miles by Indian trail from Fort Pitt, the nearest American settlement. Nevertheless, it was his, without competing American claims, without Indian complaint, without conflicting surveys. His nearest Indian neighbor was an extended Mohawk family also displaced from their eastern New York home. The nearest Indian power was Cornplanter, living on the border of Pennsylvania and New York, the traditional chief of the Allegheny Senecas, now an old man tired of war and determined to live in peace with the new American settlers.

This is not to say that Meadville was born without strife and hard work. The British were still at Fort Detroit, offering to the western Indian nations and the displaced Delawares bounty money for scalps and captives from the American frontier. In 1792, the surveys began that would transfer land surrounding the Mead tracts to speculators, veterans, and land companies and bring scrupulous and unscrupulous agents to the town. There were roads, mills, churches, and schools to build. There was government to establish and courts to seat. There were settlers to find, artisans to recruit, and trade with the distant cash markets at Pittsburgh, Philadelphia, and New Orleans to establish.

In 1813, one last threat from the British came with the appearance on Lake Erie, 35 miles to Meadville's north, of a British fleet, the symbol of the pincer campaign proposed to regain the American states for the British. In his last major service to his community, 62-year-old Mead signed on as a major general of the American land forces for defense against the expected British invasion. He oversaw a camp of 3,000 militia forces gathered at Meadville from the western counties to support General Harrison in Ohio and the post at Fort Niagara, managed the supply of Commodore Perry's tiny fleet building at Presqu'ile, recruited soldiers as marines to man it and to caisson it over the bar and out of Misery Bay, all while keeping the peace at home.

# One

# Public Spaces, Public Faces

Like most towns of its age, Meadville is visually defined by the public places it has built. David Mead, a true son of Connecticut, included a green, public square in his first 1792 survey. Roger Alden, a Yale graduate and first agent of the Holland Land Company in Meadville, endorsed this decision and enlarged upon it. As seen in Sherman Day's 1840s woodcut of early Meadville and in John Reynolds' sketches of Water Street homes, the citizens planted trees along their corduroyed streets from the earliest days.

From the 1804 log courthouse and the 1814 arsenal, the public buildings and spaces reflected the residents' expectations for their city. Each succeeding courthouse was more impressive, each city hall reflected a growth in stature, and each firehouse reflected its volunteers' pride. As the city spread east from French Creek, parks and trees accompanied new buildings. Specimen trees from bald cypress to gingko biloba to copper beech competed for attention. Allegheny College and later the Meadville Theological School both created parklike campuses for their students. The city's Market House was surrounded by a flagged and later bricked square. Public schools were set in generous lawns and surrounded by trees, and the cemeteries were landscaped as gardens and planted with rhododendrons for impressive early summer displays. In the 1930s, public arboretums were planted at Shadybrook and Ellsworth parks and on Allegheny's campus. The early concern for civic beauty continues with green ways and pedestrian ways wreathing the city's neighborhoods with natural waterways and ravines.

In 1800, the state legislature, following completion of surveys, divided the northwest frontier in preparation for the expected influx of settlers. Mercer, Venango, Warren, and Erie counties were created with a shared administrative center and court at Meadville in Crawford County. The first courthouse, built in 1804, was a two-story log structure, which served not only justice, but as the meeting room for initiating major endeavors. Here the plans for the Academy were made; the call for Timothy Alden to lead a new college issued; the nation's third oldest chamber of commerce was formed; and the strategy for acquiring the Beaver & Lake Erie arm of the Pennsylvania Canal system was completed. This plaque was cast for the 1938 sesquicentennial celebration. It also honors the 1842 creation of the primary election system.

As each county grew, individual courthouses were erected, and the judge for the northwest judicial district rode circuit between them. William Strickland of Philadelphia designed Meadville's new courthouse, erected in 1825. The Greek Revival brick structure, seen here at the left with its bell tower, faced the public square, where twice yearly the county militia drilled and where drovers rested their cattle, mules, and pigs as they walked to distant markets. In this 1840s view by Sherman Day, churches and a hotel join the courthouse to dominate the town center.

Trees have replaced cattle on the public square as the milkman makes his rounds. Old Stone (Methodist) Church draws the eye in this *c.* 1860 glass plate image by Charles Forker. (S.D. Clark collection.)

In 1867, a new courthouse was planned, a massive Victorian structure that would fill the block between Center and Cherry Streets. It is seen here in an engraving from the 1876 county atlas, with Justice rising from the clock tower. For the first time, county offices were under the same roof as the county court, whose bench now served only Crawford County.

The community gathers at Diamond Park to see their menfolk depart for the Spanish-American War.

As the public square became Diamond Park, Meadville increasingly focused on added commemorative statuary. In 1888, as the city celebrated the centennial of its founding, a statue of the pioneer was dedicated. The man in hunting shirt and buckskin leggings, carrying a long rifle, evoked the memory of David Mead. The monument was erected on May 12, 1888 to "mark the hundredth anniversary of the settlement of Crawford County and the founding of Meadville PA."

Erected in 1890 and dedicated in 1891, this memorial is made to the soldiers and sailors who served in the Civil War, "our Loyal Sons." Supposedly modeled on Samuel Pfeiffer, a color-bearer of the 150th Regiment, Pennsylvania Volunteers who fell at Gettysburg, the statue salutes all 1861–1865 service members from across the county. The chase gun and cannonballs were later additions and, today, are favored climbing places for children.

The first of the statuary for the newly named Diamond Park was the Shippen Fountain. It was donated in 1868 by Evans Shippen, son of the 6th Judicial District's third judge Henry Shippen. An architectural ironwork foundry owner, Evans Shippen gave this elegant Italianate fountain to set the tone for future growth. The fencing was a later addition, required to keep wandering children and dogs from the pool.

Heroes were found not only in wars; the city's volunteer fire companies had served the community since the earliest days of bucket brigades. In 1915, when the city authorized a full-time, paid automotive department, the volunteer hose, hook and ladder, and pumper companies erected this monument facing south down Center Street toward the new Central Station. (1954 Reed McCaskey photograph.)

Music and public celebration have been an important part of the city's life, and as Diamond Park grew more formal and sylvan, it attracted uses that were more ceremonial. This gazebo hosted band concerts and community events.

Today the tradition continues and the Dexter Bulen Memorial Gazebo, which provides on-site storage space, lighting, and power for today's activities, has replaced the Victorian gazebo.

The High Victorian Crawford County Courthouse dominated Diamond Park, Meadville's public square, for nearly 90 years. Its gravitas stemmed from its judicial and law enforcement responsibilities. Pennsylvania's counties had limited roles to play, and poorhouse and bridge

maintenance, elections, and support of the land and court records keeping were the primary duties of county commissioners until after World War II.

In the early 1950s, county government reluctantly concluded that the courthouse no longer had the physical capacity to provide the services now required of it. The north and south wings were extended forward, an addition was built along Chancery Lane at the rear, and, in a style reminiscent of the 1825 courthouse, room was made for a second courtroom and hearing rooms, and for a growing range of public agency services.

This night view of the central tower block of the remodeled building emphasizes the vertical and spare vision of the reconstruction. Today, the central block with its clock tower continues to look out over Diamond Park; it is a dominant, but not dominating presence.

While the new courthouse lacked the ornate Victorian facade, it reached for a decorative interpretation of the area's history. Flanking the great front doors, two bas-relief panels, created and sculpted by Allegheny College art professor Carl Heeschen, summarize the county's accomplishments. Their text reads: "Early circuit judges used a log courthouse built in 1804, replaced by a handsome new edifice in 1825. The courthouse next built in 1867 is still preserved to a large extent in the present structure. The Drake Well near Titusville, an event that revolutionized transportation and industry throughout the world. Pioneer of the great zipper industry. Modern factories stand among productive farms, woodlands and pastures."

The city and county have shared the public square space of Diamond Park, but Meadville retained for itself some special spaces. Nearer the business district and the industrial corridor of the railroads in Mead Park by the Erie Railroad station, the 1910 city hall supported the limited public services of the early 20th century.

Times changed for cities, too. In 1973, as the city entered into urban renewal and modernized water and sewer services, as district justices replaced justice of the peace and alderman's courts, and as expanding city limits and changing police needs required larger safety forces, a new city hall was designed at the arterial highway's Arch Street entrance to the downtown. Its council chambers and meeting rooms offer a warmer welcome to citizens participating in local government.

From Meadville's earliest days, volunteer associations had provided fire protection to the city. Neighborhood firehouses sheltered the equipment and provided social rooms for the members.

Although the volunteer companies survived, they soon gave precedence to the full-time forces, as here, where Hope Hose and the Meadville Fire Department pose at the beginning of the 20th century.

In earlier days the fire horses had their stables in city hall, but they were put out to pasture in 1915, when the city switched to a new motorized fleet and a full-time, paid department. Central Station was another signal of the prosperity of the community. Many of the volunteer hose, pumper, and ladder departments survived, serving as fire auxiliaries and special services units.

Following the War of 1812, the state built this arsenal to supply basic defense needs in case of future emergencies. The building was well fitted out, but its arms, forges, powder canisters, and military materiel were never needed. The building itself was used sporadically as extra classroom space for Allegheny College and as a segregated school for the Negro population, which was centered around the North and Randolph Streets area. In 1870, the new North Ward School was built on the site.

About 1900, a new armory was built facing Diamond Park. Later remodeled, it still serves as the home of the National Guard unit.

For 60 years, the town had shared David Mead's family cemetery, just east of his Randolph Street home. By the 1850s, a burgeoning population and new state regulations forced the creation of a new community cemetery outside city limits, and Greendale Cemetery was created. Seen here in a glass plate stereo view by Dunn, the new burying ground was laid out on a rise at the eastern edge of the city, handsomely landscaped as a park, and planted with rhododendrons, which still flourish today. The stone gateway welcomed visitors through triad pedestrian and carriage arches, and curving lanes ran beside the ravine among the plots.

As Meadville was the county seat and market center for the region, citizens had been calling for a market house since 1815, but other priorities always seemed to overtake the need. In 1870, following the failure of two private sector market efforts, the city cleared a square in the downtown business district and built a handsome brick market house. From the beginning it was a success, acting not only as a center for area farmers and craftsmen to sell their products but also as a commercial generator for the downtown retail, hospitality, and banking businesses.

Today, on the east plaza, a Trail of History marker commemorates Market Square's role.

Enlarged in 1917, the Market House now also sheltered fledgling social service agencies such as the Red Cross and the Tuberculosis Society, provided meeting rooms and comfort facilities, and housed the nascent Farm Bureau services of the early 20th century.

As the world grew more motorized, the Market House flourished and the commercial district around it prospered accordingly.

Following World War II, the Market House stumbled, finding it difficult to identify its role in a world of "super" markets and produce imported by refrigerated trucks. The Pennsylvania Department of Labor and Industry descended to require major renovations, and the Chamber of Commerce called for a parking garage in its place.

The 100-year-old market "put it to the people" who voted with volunteer services and generous donations to revitalize what for many of them defined the heart of Meadville. The building was renovated, the square upgraded, and a new rebirth of downtown began. By 1997, local artist Leslie Blake recorded the renewed gathering place quality of the market, and as the city entered the 21st century, new commercial development appeared around the Market Square area.

In 1988, the city celebrated its bicentennial. From May 12 to July 4, a series of entertainment events, community activities, school curriculum development, and facade face-lifting involved all the city's residents. A lasting contribution was achieved in the recreated David Mead Log Cabin, which was created entirely by volunteers, furnished by Antique Study Club, incorporated into the elementary school curriculum, and developed as a historic site and community park. Located along French Creek, with a boat access, picnic facility, interpretive cabin, health walk, and native plantings, the park was renamed the Kenneth A Beers Bicentennial Park in memory of the dedicated city engineer who led the project.

One of the first two attorneys admitted to the bar of Crawford County in 1800, Henry Baldwin was appointed in 1830 to the U.S. Supreme Court by Pres. Andrew Jackson. In 1842, Justice Baldwin and his wife returned to Meadville, where he built this antebellum Greek Revival home overlooking French Creek. His death in 1844 left his wife with an unfinished building and more house and less income than she needed, and she sold the home to her nephew William Reynolds. In the 60 years Reynolds and his family lived here, he continued to improve and beautify the house and its grounds and, today, it is the museum of the Crawford County Historical Society.

# Two

# Getting Here
# from Anywhere

When in 1753 the 21-year-old George Washington made his embassy up French Creek to France's Fort LeBoeuf, he had followed the network of Indian paths that connected the far-flung limits of the Iroquois Confederacy.

Travel routes had not improved 35 years later when, subsequent to the nation's independence, David Mead set out to take up his western lands, following the road map of Washington's journal to the rich meadows of the upper Ohio Valley.

Mead and his companions found themselves in a remote area. The confluence of the Cussewago and French Creeks was nearly 50 water miles from the nearest American fort at Franklin on the Allegheny River and 100 land miles from Fort Pitt, or Pittsburgh as it came to be called. Neither trip was easy.

While water transportation was generally faster and easier, French Creek was high and rough in winter and spring, full of meanders and rocky bottoms. Come summer its flow decreased until no keelboat could travel it, and flatboats were often left aground in shallows. The Indian paths could not support wagon or carriage travel, and the abundance of streams and wetlands made road building problematic, limited to following the high lip of the creek's escarpment. Goods were packed in on horseback or on foot, and products such as salt, grain, lumber, and potash could be shipped out only when the creek was in spate in spring and late fall.

Transport of men and goods, imports and exports, were to remain a constant challenge for the farmers and manufacturers of Meadville.

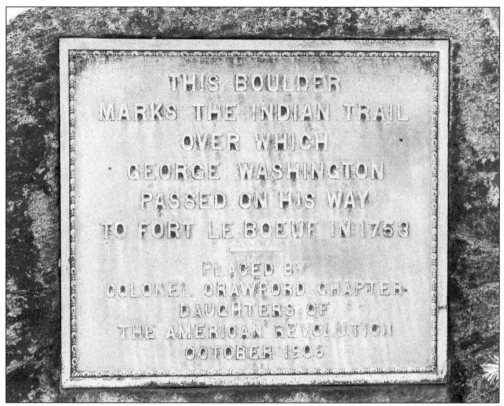

THIS BOULDER
MARKS THE INDIAN TRAIL
OVER WHICH
GEORGE WASHINGTON
PASSED ON HIS WAY
TO FORT LE BOEUF IN 1753

PLACED BY
COLONEL CRAWFORD CHAPTER
DAUGHTERS OF
THE AMERICAN REVOLUTION
OCTOBER 1906

The Iroquois had walked this path for centuries before George Washington followed it to Fort LeBoeuf and, for Meadville's early settlers, it became Water Street.

This cased daguerreotype is of John Reynolds's home on Water Street, taken probably in 1863. Of particular interest is its view of the Plank Road, a revolutionary paved turnpike north to Edinboro. Also in evidence are the city's wooden sidewalks. The trees appear to be Lombard poplars, the first visual evidence we have of what was a local 19th-century obsession—the nurture of specimen trees not native to the area. In competitive near frenzy, leading citizens planted gingko biloba, copper and purple beech, magnolia, bald cypress, and other exotics.

This reproduction of an early painting presents the c. 1810 toll bridge over French Creek at Drover's Way, now Mercer Street. The bridge was erected by Dr. Kennedy to replace the ferry that had previously operated at the narrows of French Creek there. Accidents took the life of at least one man and of several horses and cattle. The cornerstone was salvaged when the county later rebuilt the bridge and it is now on display at the Baldwin-Reynolds House Museum.

Meadville's streets have sometimes suggested the expression "clear sailing," as this 1913 flood photograph shows. The portico on the left is the entrance to the Lafayette Hotel, at the corner of Water and Chestnut Streets; the hotel burned in 1955. To the east is the Smith Block, which still stands, its 1900s Toggery advertising today visible on its north Market Square facade.

Early street paving was done by hand, with little machine support in evidence. As cars became more common, cement bases for brick streets required the "sophisticated" equipment seen in this view of early street crews at work, probably in the city's Fifth Ward.

Early cars faltered at steep grades, such as Route 322 on its way from Meadville to Conneaut Lake and Ohio. Here, the steam shovel cleans up after blasting has lowered the crest of Gable Hill. Most of the equipment was motorized, but a few horses still pulled their weight

The early mud, plank, and gravel roads eventually evolved into concrete thoroughfares such as this stretch of U.S. 19, approaching the city. This probably staged shot c. 1926 emphasizes state trooper patrols and safety for school buses on these new relatively high-speed (45 to 50 mph) traffic arteries.

Forty-five years later, the Meadville arterial is shown at its October 13, 1973 dedication, its function to divert truck and through traffic around the center city. In the vehicle Jacob Kassab, Pennsylvania Department of Transportation secretary, is joined by Miss Crawford County Frances Logue and Charles "Sky" Wyatt, owner of Meadville's first Chevrolet dealership.

Captain Richard Patch, a keelboater and waterman on the Allegheny River, retired to Meadville in 1797 and settled down as an innkeeper. His family of five daughters made advantageous marriages in the increasingly prosperous community.

The Patch Tavern stood on the southwest corner of Chestnut and Market Streets until the early 1900s, when it was razed to make way for a bank.

The unpredictable water levels of French Creek, seen on the left, did not make the stream viable for commercial travel and, in 1827, ground was broken for the French Creek Feeder Canal. Here, the camera looks north along the towpath toward Daniel Shryock's home. Shryock had prospered from salt-producing brine wells until, in deepening them in 1819, he struck oil and ruined his primary product.

Capt. James Dickson made a career on the canal. His boat is seen here just south of the North Street bridge. Walls and property lines askew can still trace the course of the canal, which cuts diagonally through the city.

In the heart of the city, a man sculls his boat across the canal basin in front of David Dick's home, at today's Cherry and Market Streets. The man may well be David Dick himself, said to be so restless that on one occasion he started walking rather than wait for a tardy Pittsburgh-bound stagecoach, and reached the city before it did. The small black child seems to be sitting on a wheeled carrier, perhaps an early boat trailer. Dick was an inveterate inventor who, with a Mr. Blanchard, engineered the *Allegheny*—the first sternwheeler steamboat—and later won the gold Council Medal at London's 1851 Crystal Palace exhibition for his eccentric gear press. At the time of his death in 1870, he had taken out the first patents on an aerostatic engine, a precursor to the internal combustion engine, inspired by the oil boom in eastern Crawford County.

40

Basins for industry and heavy goods depots marked the course of the canal as it passed through the city. Here, the canal passes Athens Mills as it enters Meadville from the north. On the right, French Creek flows in its original bed at about 12-foot lower elevation.

Slow travel, heavy maintenance costs, and winter closings made the canal an unsatisfactory answer to the long term shipping needs of Meadville's foundries and agricultural industries, and it closed in 1871. This boat livery above Race Street remained, providing pleasure seekers with rentals for summer days.

Water levels of French Creek have always been unpredictable, but low dams created slack water areas, where teakettle steamers, such as this one accompanied by sculls and loaded with summer pleasure seekers, could take cool water excursions to picnic sites upstream. In spite of the creek's obnoxious habits of winter flooding and summer low water, area residents have been largely good stewards of their waterway. Today, the Nature Conservancy calls it one of the "last great places" in the United States, and "the most biologically diverse stream in Pennsylvania." The Audubon Society has identified three major bird habitats in the French Creek watershed. A total of 27 varieties of mussels, 80 species of fish (including rare darters), and a unique hellbender remain much as George Washington and his party must have found them in 1753.

In 1864, William Reynolds's Atlantic & Great Western Railroad linked the Port of New York to St. Louis via the eastern New York & Lake Erie and the western Ohio & Missouri Railroads. The meeting point was the Atlantic & Great Western station, hotel, and yards at Meadville. In the January 19, 1864 *New York Daily Tribune*, Horace Greeley gave extravagant praise to this halfway point, as he continued to urge young men to "Go West." The hotel wing, just seen behind the covered track station and train, boasted gardens complete with fountains and walkways, and rental carriages so that passengers could start the next day of their trip refreshed.

This engraving of the McHenry House restaurant conveys a feeling for the size and scope of the facility. Its menu measured up to the room's grandeur.

43

Soon to be integrated as the Erie Railroad, the Atlantic & Great Western-New York & Lake Erie-Ohio & Missouri merged road was made viable by the Atlantic & Great Western link that ran from Salamanca, New York, to Marion, Ohio. Completed in October 1862 as track was laid from Ohio east and New York State west, the Atlantic & Great Western New York-Pennsylvania-and-Ohio section bypassed the Pennsylvania Railroad's monopoly on Pennsylvania trackage and opened a new route to Chicago and the West. The first engine to make the connection

was the *William Reynolds*, its maiden trip the 80-mile Meadville-to-Corry round-trip, with stops for celebration, in 13 hours. The Meadville station was 327 feet long and 127 feet wide, and its "big depot, handsome, well lighted and orderly offices and above all its unequalled hotel," had, according to the *Crawford Democrat*, "brought the luxury and magnificence of New York living" to Meadville.

Under the guidance of Don Jose de Salamanca's financing and James McHenry's engineering, the Meadville yards were fully equipped and modern in every aspect. Here, an Atlantic & Great Western locomotive rides proudly on the roundtable, which served a roundhouse said to have been the largest east of the Mississippi.

The building clearly identifies this scene in the Meadville yards of the Atlantic & Great Western. Local railroaders suggest that the two locomotives were running the gauntlet, attempting to hitch, but meeting a track apart. Accidents were not uncommon, although the wider English gauge adopted by the Atlantic & Great Western tended to lend extra stability to the rolling stock.

Between 1870 and c. 1890, the Atlantic & Great Western ran between French Creek and the abandoned French Creek Feeder Canal, utilizing the canal's towpath as a roadbed on its spur to Franklin and the oil fields. This view was taken between Meadville and Shaw's Landing.

Keystone View Company,

Meadville, Penna.

23—Boat riding in N. Y., P. & O. Machine shop.

The Atlantic & Great Western's proximity to French Creek put it in harm's way when floods hit. This Keystone View stereo card documents the extent to which water would rise in the line's New York-Pennsylvania-and-Ohio Division yards. The consolidation of the various companies and sectors into the Erie Railroad came shortly after this period, although the property ownerships were never totally disentangled.

Meadville's leaders always saw competition as a healthy thing. While the Atlantic & Great Western Railroad provided service between New York and Chicago, access to the Pennsylvania Railroad and its Philadelphia terminus was still desirable. The Meadville-to-Linesville Railway initially made the Pennsylvania Railroad connection. Later, the line found its profit in a north–south orientation, which linked Pittsburgh to Lake Erie at Conneaut, Ohio. Through a series of reorganizations, it eventually became the Bessemer and Lake Erie, the road of the steel industry, carrying ore from the Great Lakes to Pittsburgh. In this 1898 view, the Bessemer station is crowded, as residents come to see their men off to the Spanish-American War.

In the postwar years, railroaders, fresh from the passenger traffic and heavy freight cartage of the early 1940s, saw no limit on their future. This futuristic GM engine was one of many dream machines that paused in Meadville.

This 1950s aerial photograph gives a comprehensive view of the postwar rail yard operation at Meadville. In the upper right, Vallonia, Meadville's Fifth Ward, west of the central cut made to straighten French Creek, was home to many Erie Railroad workers. The original beds of the French and Cussewago Creeks are defined by their tree lines, upper left, near the Meadville

Distillery buildings on Race Street. Lined up on the left, what appear to be retired steam engines await attention. The mainline tracks cut diagonally from the middle right to the center foreground of the photograph, where cars parked on McHenry Street indicate the presence of the passenger station to their left.

Following World War II, the Erie Railroad, like its competitors, looked confidently forward to a profitable future and began substantial investment in new rolling stock. Loyal to its Meadville roots, it launched the *William Reynolds*, one of its new modern sleepers, in 1949. Present for the event were John Bainer; Mrs. Hayward; R.E. Woodruff, Erie president; Mrs. Johnson; Mrs. John E. Reynolds, widow of William Reynolds's son; Mrs. Bainer; Mrs. Bates; Paul W. Johnson, Erie operations vice president; James R. Shryock, descendant of the Atlantic & Great Western (Pennsylvania division's) first president and brother of Mrs. Reynolds; Robert S. Bates, publisher of the *Meadville Tribune*; and G.E. Hayward, the mayor of Meadville.

For 30 years, from the 1890s through the 1920s, another style of track travel captured Meadville's imagination and its capital. As a secondary transport linkage throughout the county and to Lake Erie, urban and interurban cars drew large numbers of riders. Tracks were laid throughout the city, shown here at Water and Chestnut Streets, where the urban lines turned west for one block to the carbarns and the Erie Railroad station. The streetlight illuminating the intersection was one of a series which kept the constable busy; like the old Christmas tree lights, when one went, the whole string went and the constable was expected to identify the culprit and replace it.

By 1890, no new business seemed able to get under way without a formal photograph of all the people, who today remain unidentified. The Meadville Traction employees pose in front of the carbarns on lower Chestnut Street next to the railroad station and the electric generating plant. While the urban lines were getting under way, construction was going forward on interurban lines intended to link Meadville to Conneaut Lake and Linesville, Saegertown, and Cambridge Springs and, eventually, to Titusville's budding trolley system, thereby serving most if not all of Crawford County's 1,000 square miles.

To stimulate maximum ridership, Meadville Traction invested in Oakwood Park, a family destination in the late 1800s and early 1900s. The park featured a spring dance floor ballroom, an artificial lake with rental rowing boats, walking paths, the area's first movies or "flickers," a pavilion, dining facilities, special events such as balloon ascensions, and mineral water.

The city's system intensively covered the town. As this trolley's signboard indicates, the Randolph line ran to Greendale, the city's cemetery.

The best service in the world could not, however, beat out the new buses, which moved more quickly and could be routed more flexibly. The Northwest Interurban Railway and the new bus company pose together, like two runners at the starting line. By the close of the 1920s, the trolley system had ceased even to carry freight or mail.

The automobile came to Meadville in 1901 through the inventive genius of two teenage boys. William Thompson and Harold Kantner collaborated on creating this three-wheeled runabout, which might make it up College Hill only in reverse, but which certainly got them attention.

#5 BOAT
28' GAR WOOD 500HP LIBERTY ENGINE
CLOCKED SPEED 65 MPH

Bill Thompson went on to design and build boats. His 28-foot Gar Wood hull with a 500-horsepower Liberty airplane engine ran on Conneaut Lake at 65 mph.

Harold Kantner turned to flying, perhaps inspired by the 1911 landing of the Vin Fizz in Meadville as it made the first transcontinental flight. Calbraith Perry Rodgers, who aimed to win a $1,000 prize by making the West Coast from Long Island in a month, had piloted the Vin Fizz. It took him 45 days, but he refused to quit short of his destination.

Harold Kantner bought the elegant Renault he pilots up Park Avenue with the prize money won in a Manhattan Island air race. He went on to train pilots for Pancho Villa and for the World War I Italian Air Force, and worked for Curtiss as a test pilot and in barnstorming promotional flights.

Harold Kantner was not the only one who was bitten by the urge to fly. Not one but two airports sprang up on the outskirts of town in the 1920s and sports pilots, both men and women, joined clubs and racing leagues. The practical aspects such as airfreight and airmail are demonstrated in this view.

Today, Port Meadville and its B.J. Smith terminal are the base for corporate Learjets but remain home to the recreational aircraft and historic models of the enthusiasts.

Early flying was not without its hazards, and this photograph from the H.E. Ellsworth collection documents the last landing of Air Ship 291. The February 26, 1923, flight from Bellefonte to Cleveland reportedly lost visual contact with the ground due to heavy fog. Elmer G. Leonardt, an Army Air Corps veteran, had flown for the Air Mail Service since September 1919 until he circled Fred Crawford's Custead pasture in an attempted landing. According to the official report, he was carrying only 78 pounds of mail, some of which was recovered and forwarded to Cleveland by train with the pilot's body.

Shortly after the Civil War, Samuel Sylvester "Vet" Thurston moved to Meadville from Guys Mills and became a hotel keeper and a balloonist. His balloon, the Meadville, flew for every local celebration, and he set speed and distance records in national competitions. Here, his son Alic flies from Market Square c. 1895.

Power poles clearly were climbed without alarm, as these balloon watchers demonstrate, again at Market Square.

# *Three*

# LEADERS AND
# INNOVATORS

The success of new frontier settlements depended heavily on local leadership. If any one characteristic can be attributed to David Mead, it was a determination to succeed in this western wilderness.

The Mead family had originally left Fairfield, Connecticut, for Dutchess County, east of the Hudson, in New York. When Connecticut opened lands that it also claimed under its royal charter in the Wyoming Valley of Pennsylvania, the Meads moved on there, choosing this time to file under a Pennsylvania title. Again, when contested, their title failed, but the Pennsylvania courts awarded them lands over the Appalachians as compensation. Following the Revolutionary War's close, the Meads made their way west, determined that this would be their final move.

Four Mead brothers, John, Joseph, Darius Jr., and David, led the first party of settlers in 1788. They settled on land noted by George Washington on his 1753 embassy to the French at Fort LeBoeuf, land that was within a day's trip of the newly garrisoned Fort Franklin, at which Mead's brother-in-law William Wilson was to become the trader in 1792.

Mead's party was soon followed by an agent of the Holland Land Company, which had secured rights to sell millions of acres of frontier land. Maj. Roger Alden, a Yale graduate and Revolutionary War veteran, was a congenial and intelligent co-promoter who worked well with Mead as they built mills, schools, and trails, and recruited artisans and farmers to settle the area.

Quality recruiters attracted quality settlers, and an educated and innovative leadership corps emerged, one that set high goals for the future of the town.

This glass plate print is apparently of a Mead family reunion, posed on the southwest lawn of the home built for David Mead in 1797. None of the participants are identified except for the portrait prominently displayed in the right center of the image. The only portrait of David Mead, known to have existed well into the 20th century, the picture has disappeared except as

recorded in this probably 1860s view. The house still stands, considerably remodeled *c.* 1915, at the corner of Randolph, Market, Water, and Terrace Streets on the old Venango Path, and is currently undergoing restoration.

Originally assigned to its Philadelphia office, Dutch-born Harm Jan Huidekoper was sent to Meadville by the European-owned Holland Land Company to evaluate the problems encountered in promoting and exploiting the millions of acres of land it had bought for speculation in western Pennsylvania and New York. Huidekoper replaced the original agent, Revolutionary War hero Maj. Roger Alden, married Rebecca Colqhoun (Calhoun), and became an active if contrarian participant in the area's growth. He established an Independent Congregational church, a nontraditional college-theological school, a competing rail link, and several family businesses. In 1836, he bought out the remainder of the Holland Land Company's properties in western Pennsylvania, which the family, operating as the Huidekoper Land Company, continued to sell.

Huidekoper set a European standard of living for himself and his family, as reflected in this well-sprung carriage and matched team. The outfit stands in front of the old Holland Land Company offices on Water Street, next to the family's Pomona Hall residence. Following Huidekoper's death in 1836, his sons chose to build much larger and more elaborate homes on upper Chestnut Street and donated land just east of their properties to establish a campus for the Meadville Theological School in 1844.

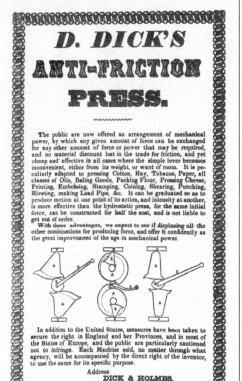

## D. DICK'S
## ANTI-FRICTION
## PRESS.

The public are now offered an arrangement of mechanical power, by which any given amount of force can be exchanged for any other amount of force or power that may be required, and no material discount lost in the trade for friction, and yet cheap and effective in all cases where the simple lever becomes inconvenient, either from its weight, or want of room. It is peculiarly adapted to pressing Cotton, Hay, Tobacco, Paper, all classes of Oils, Baling Goods, Packing Flour, Pressing Cheese, Printing, Embossing, Stamping, Coining, Shearing, Punching, Riveting, making Lead Pipe, &c. It can be graduated so as to produce motion at one point of its action, and intensity at another, is more effective than the hydrostatic press, for the same initial force, can be constructed for half the cost, and is not liable to get out of order.

With these advantages, we expect to see it displacing all the other combinations for producing force, and offer it confidently as the great improvement of the age in mechanical power.

In addition to the United States, measures have been taken to secure the right in England and her Provinces, and in most of the States of Europe, and the public are particularly cautioned not to infringe. Each Machine sold, no matter through what agency, will be accompanied by the direct right of the inventor, to use the same for its specific purpose.

Address
**DICK & HOLMES,**
MEADVILLE, CRAWFORD CO., PA.

OLIVER & BROTHER'S Steam Press, 59 Nassau-Street, corner of Fulton, N. Y.

David Dick never stopped looking for new and better ways to do ordinary things, but his best- known and most financially rewarding patent was the Anti-Friction Press, an eccentric geared device that could pull stumps from the ground or ships into dry dock. He and his brothers were partners in Dick, Fisk & Company, later Meadville's Phoenix Foundry. The Council Medal, cast by the Royal Mint in 1851 for the Industrial Exhibition, Crystal Palace, shows Victoria and Albert on the obverse and bears the motto "Est etiam in magno quaedam respublica mundo" on the reverse. The advertising piece puffs off the many uses of the invention while issuing fair warning that it has been patented worldwide.

David Dick was the third of five boys born to William and Anna McGunnegle Dick, the first after their move to Meadville in 1795. Their family's living room had been pressed into use as the venue for the first county court, held in 1800. Each boy had gone on to success as banker, businessman, soldier, or manufacturer. David Dick married Lydia Colqhoun (Calhoun) sister of Rebecca Huidekoper. He traveled widely, lectured at the newly organized Smithsonian Institution, and with his brothers manufactured his inventions at the Phoenix Foundry.

This elevation from 1861 shows the south facade of the Meadville station and McHenry House. Above it, a pencil sketch of the east facade, facing the town, offers a concept of the massive impact the original station had on the rapidly growing city.

Financing for the New York-Pennsylvania-and-Ohio-incorporated Atlantic & Great Western railroads was hard to come by as the Civil War opened. William Reynolds led a committee to Europe where, while awaiting a meeting with Spain's Don Jose de Salamanca and the Duc de Navarre in Paris, he sat to have his likeness taken and reproduced as *cartes de visite*.

A native of Connecticut, Henry Baldwin was one of the first two attorneys to be accepted at the Crawford County bar in 1800. Following his marriage to Sally Ellicott, sister of John Reynolds's wife Jane Judith, he moved on to Pittsburgh where he became a foundry owner and participated in politics. His support of Andrew Jackson earned him an appointment to the U.S. Supreme Court, where he served from 1830 to 1844. In 1842, the couple returned to Meadville to build what they intended to be their retirement home.

Following Henry Baldwin's 1844 death, William Reynolds, Sally Baldwin's nephew, acquired the home, shown here c. 1888, with a view of Lord's Pond, site of the War of 1812 militia encampment.

One of the earliest and most defining decisions made by the residents of Meadville was to establish a college so that their children could be educated on the frontier as they would have been on the Atlantic seaboard. The cornerstone for the first building, Bentley Hall, was laid in 1820, and the building was completed in 1827 by David Dick.

The man whom residents chose to undertake the task of establishing the college was Timothy Alden, a descendant of John and Priscilla Alden, a Harvard graduate, and a cousin of Roger Alden who was then a congressman. In June 1815, 25 years after the city's founding, subscription books were opened, the first college faculty appointed, and a charter sought. Alden returned to the East to solicit gifts, especially books for the college's library. More than $10,000 and 5,000 books resulted.

As the struggle to establish Allegheny College proved too much for Alden, an inquiry came from the growing Methodist Episcopal church as to whether the college would accept its involvement. Alden, a Presbyterian, could not continue under Methodist control. In 1833, management of the school transferred to the Pittsburgh Conference, although many local residents of varying religious affiliation remained on the board. The Reverend Martin Ruter, a vigorous supporter of popular education, was chosen as the second president, and 100 students were enrolled.

In 1854, the college's second building was dedicated and named after Martin Ruter, its second president, who had died in 1838.

Two early settlers of great influence in widely differing ways were Thomas Atkinson and Cornelius Van Horn. Thomas Atkinson (left) arrived in Meadville in 1804 and, in partnership with W. Brendle, set up a press and commenced publication of the *Crawford Weekly Messenger* in January 1805 The only newspaper in northwestern Pennsylvania, it had wide circulation and great influence. Atkinson was active in the creation of the Society for the Encouragement of Domestic Manufactures and the Useful Arts (recognized as the nation's third oldest chamber of commerce) in 1807 and served as the borough's first burgess in 1823.

Cornelius Van Horn was a member of David Mead's original party in 1788, a veteran of the Revolutionary War. During the early years, 1790 to 1795, when the British at Fort Detroit were still offering the western nations scalp fees on American frontier settlers, Van Horn accepted the task of raising and leading a local militia force to protect the Meadville settlement

Roger Alden had fought at Lexington and Concord and had served through the Revolutionary War to the last shot fired at Yorktown. He later served as a secretary at Congress and as principal clerk in the Department of State. In 1795, he came to the frontier as agent for the Holland Land Company and later served as state representative and U.S. congressman before taking semiretirement in 1825 as quartermaster at West Point.

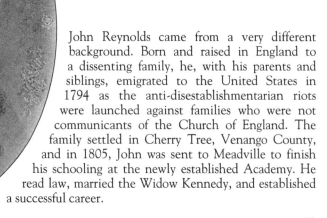

John Reynolds came from a very different background. Born and raised in England to a dissenting family, he, with his parents and siblings, emigrated to the United States in 1794 as the anti-disestablishmentarian riots were launched against families who were not communicants of the Church of England. The family settled in Cherry Tree, Venango County, and in 1805, John was sent to Meadville to finish his schooling at the newly established Academy. He read law, married the Widow Kennedy, and established a successful career.

When artist and ornithologist John James Audubon found himself stranded without funds in Meadville in 1824, he refilled his wallet doing charcoal and pastel drawings of local dignitaries. A surviving example is this portrait of Pieter Huidekoper, younger brother of Harm Jan, whose visit coincided with Audubon's involuntary sojourn.

Local men reached national prominence in unpredictable ways. Joseph Camp Griffith Kennedy, half-brother to William Reynolds, was a mathematician of international reputation in the fields of statistics and theory. In 1850, he became the superintendent of the Federal Census, devising more comprehensive and precise methods for the enumeration. It was a task he continued for the 1860 census, surviving the changing political scene on his own merits.

Crawford County was considered a Democratic anti-Federalist stronghold and even through the Civil War a strong undertow of Democratic support remained. The *Crawford Democrat* ran a stop-press notice of a poisoning attempt on Pres. Abraham Lincoln in the summer of 1864, which apparently triggered this message scrawled on a window of the McHenry House hotel. While John Wilkes Booth was a fairly frequent customer of the hotel as he made his way to Franklin to pursue his oil field speculation, he was not registered at this date. After Lincoln's assassination in 1865, the pane of glass was removed and framed with an earlier Booth registration signature and was for many years displayed at the Ford Theater museum in Washington, D.C.

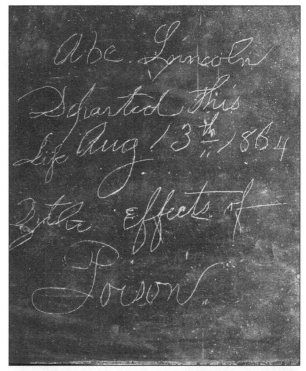

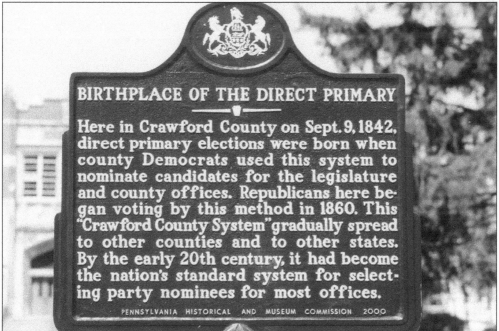

Politics were meat and bread to local residents. In 1842, following a totally unexpected defeat by the Whigs (who were no longer Federalists but not yet Republicans), the fragmented Democrat-Republican party (not to be confused with either the Democrats *or* the Republicans of today) undertook a preelection vote to determine their candidates for county offices. In so doing, they created the primary election system as a way to choose the most electable slate.

Growing up in the Oil Creek Valley, Ida Tarbell knew the sins of Standard Oil firsthand. Following graduation from Allegheny College in 1880 and an apprenticeship at the Chautauquan Magazine, published in Meadville, she moved on to become one of the first and greatest investigative journalists, working primarily for McClure's Magazine.

From the day that Jennet Finney moved in to a cabin abandoned for the winter by William Gill and claimed it as her own, local women had been independent movers and shakers. Alice Bentley (right) was for 20 years a teacher and then a successful insurance agent but, feeling that the results of the 1920 election showed none of the elevating effects expected by the addition of women's votes, she ran for the state legislature and won three terms. She spent much of her remaining life working to increase the role of women in the party.

The founding of the Chautauqua Institute, in southwestern New York State, brought the Reverend Theodore Flood to Meadville, where Allegheny College was an educational bastion of the Methodist Church. He established the Chautauqua Press and published the *Chautauquan Magazine*, a part of the self-improvement, adult education outreach of the institute. Interested in all forms of community improvement, he later ran for Congress and was defeated by Franklin oil magnate Joseph Sibley.

George W Delamater was heir to an immense oil fortune derived from the Noble-Delamater Well, one of the largest producers in the history of the Oil Creek Valley. The family had been neighbors of John Brown during his decade at the New Richmond tannery, related to him by marriage, a political plus in a Republican stronghold. Entering politics, Delamater served in the state senate until 1890, when he ran for governor and was narrowly defeated.

The multitalented Tinker sisters had traveled the country with their musician father, performing in major venues from New York to Chicago. They all married Meadville husbands and settled down. Two of them gave occasional performances, but the eldest, Juvia, became a voice teacher and, in 1887, the founder of the Conservatory of Music. She remained the guiding force of the school as it became the Pennsylvania College of Music in 1911.

Dr. David Best had one son, an attorney, and four bright daughters. Two of the daughters became doctors, one became a housewife and one became the missionary wife of the bishop of Japan and Korea in 1873. Skilled in writing the Japanese language, Flora Best Harris (right) earned great respect from the Japanese people as she not only translated American hymns into Japanese but also created delicate poetry in the Japanese manner.

Raymond P. Shafer began a political career as a county district attorney and went on to become governor of Pennsylvania, a leading figure in the moderate wing of the national Republican party and counselor to Vice Pres. Nelson Rockefeller. Seen here with Pres. Dwight Eisenhower, Shafer has maintained his centrist position.

This third-generation scion of the Reynolds family was no less active or distinguished in his service to the community than were his father and grandfather. John E. Reynolds served three terms as mayor of the city, took the lead in city improvements from the Market House to the public library, and preserved both the family mansion and the family's collection of historical materials. His 1938 book *In French Creek Valley* remains one of the best resources on local history.

In the local tradition of entrepreneurship, Col. Lewis Walker took a flyer on Whitcomb Judson's "hookless fastener," shown above in bronzed shoes, to commemorate the zipper's earliest use. Walker saw the zipper's potential for clothing closures and continued to develop it  for the rag trade. Its practical development was achieved by the inventive genius of Swedish-born engineer Gideon Sundback, and the Goodrich Company coined the popular designation of "zipper" when it replaced awkward buckles with slide fasteners in snow boots.

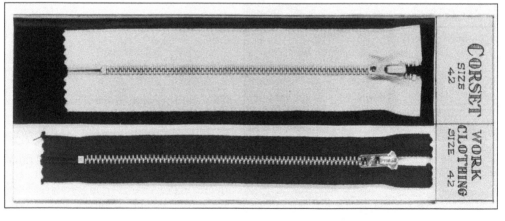

Lewis Walker, an 1877 graduate of Allegheny College and a lawyer by profession, came upon Judson's "hookless fastener" and was quick to see its potential. Investing the family's money in an industrial start-up, he began the difficult job of wooing clothing manufacturers away from buttons and snap closures. The first major breakthrough was its use on a tobacco pouch, but the Talon zipper eventually traveled into space on astronauts' flight suits.

The key to the eventual success of Talon Inc. was Gideon Sundback, a young engineer whose mechanical wizardry created the tooling necessary for the zipper's precision manufacturing. Talon's (tool and die) apprentice program eventually created a new industrial base for Meadville, the precision machining and tooling required for today's high-tech world.

An adventurous spirit set Paul Siple's feet on the path to a career as an Antarctic scientist and explorer. As a Boy Scout and Allegheny College undergraduate, Siple won the job of dog tender for Adm. Richard Byrd's 1928 expedition and, from that time on, pursued an Antarctic career. Siple's best-known contribution is the development in 1939 of wind-chill factor measurement.

Another local scientist-explorer, also an Allegheny College graduate, Robert H. Gray became the launch director at NASA's Kennedy Space Center, managing the space shuttle program.

On one of the last presidential whistle-stop campaigns, a youthful Richard Nixon drew a crowd at the Erie Railroad station siding in 1952 as he campaigned for the Eisenhower-Nixon ticket, with his wife, Pat Nixon, at his side.

Gov. Raymond P. Shafer maintained close ties with his alma mater, Allegheny College, bringing a number of outstanding national figures to the campus for graduation addresses. Here Vice Pres. Nelson Rockefeller, (left) pats a baby and greets local officials as a skeptical Spike Siegel (right), news editor for the *Meadville Tribune*, peers over his glasses and takes notes.

Not everyone featured in a photograph becomes famous. This Keystone stereo view, taken on lower Chestnut Street, records a moment of early-20th-century daily life: a newsboy wearing knickers hawks the *Evening Republican*, and a man with boater and watch fob buys a copy of the newspaper. Neither one's name has been recorded for posterity.

# Four

# INGENUITY +
# PRODUCTIVITY =
# PROSPERITY

Frontier life seems to have bred an inventive turn of mind and an entrepreneurial spirit in Meadville's residents.

Despite its remote location from major markets, Meadville businesses approached production with energy and ingenuity. From the 1790s lumber and whiskey exports rafted to Pittsburgh's 500 residents to the later agricultural products and manufactured goods shipped by water and rail, local men brought imagination and a can-do attitude to the task of building the local economy.

The Densmore brothers, James and Amos, built the first oil tanker railroad cars and made Sholes proto-typewriter a user-friendly product. Photographers Dunn and Roddy laid the groundwork for a local stereo industry, which was to become the world's largest producer of stereo views. George Dearment, an area blacksmith who made world-quality farrier's tools, saw the potential markets in the new automotive industry, and Channelock was born.

Silk mills, glass factories, cashmere woolen mills, straw paper manufacturers, locomotive and railroad car shops, agricultural field equipment, and carriages and wagon manufactories all joined the everyday production of food, hardware, and dry goods found in most small towns of the 19th and early 20th century.

Local inventions as well as under-exploited potential found elsewhere were the basis of a growth that exploded in the first two decades of the 20th century and carried Meadville through the Great Depression without bank failures or economic pain. Only the post–World War II shift to a global economy eventually, but only temporarily, slowed the city's economy.

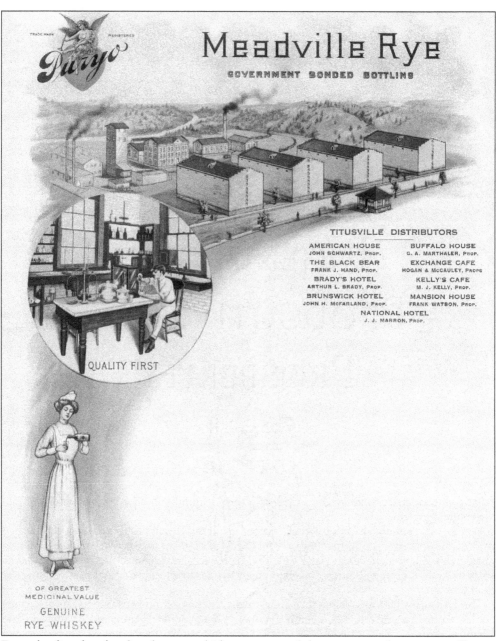

**Meadville Rye**

GOVERNMENT BONDED BOTTLING

*Purijo* TRADE MARK REGISTERED

QUALITY FIRST

OF GREATEST
MEDICINAL VALUE

GENUINE
RYE WHISKEY

**TITUSVILLE DISTRIBUTORS**

| | |
|---|---|
| AMERICAN HOUSE | BUFFALO HOUSE |
| JOHN SCHWARTZ, Prop. | G. A. MARTHALER, Prop. |
| THE BLACK BEAR | EXCHANGE CAFE |
| FRANK J. HAND, Prop. | HOGAN & McCAULEY, Props. |
| BRADY'S HOTEL | KELLY'S CAFE |
| ARTHUR L. BRADY, Prop. | M. J. KELLY, Prop. |
| BRUNSWICK HOTEL | MANSION HOUSE |
| JOHN H. McFARLAND, Prop. | FRANK WATSON, Prop. |
| NATIONAL HOTEL | |
| J. J. MARRON, Prop. | |

From the first decade of settlement, whiskey was one of the primary cash crops, an efficient way to convey abundant corn crops to market. However, rye was quickly found to be a more resilient crop and made better drinking. By 1860, a major distillery was producing some of the best rye whiskey in the country, and its headquarters was proudly displayed on its corporate stationery. Four bonded warehouses dwarf the springhouse, where the pure waters of Spring Run were diverted to the distilling process, carefully tested by the company's "scientist." The nurse measuring the medicinal dose offers an additional endorsement, which would never pass muster today. Varying sets were printed, localized to designated markets, as this sample was to Titusville. The national experiment in universal temperance known as Prohibition effectually closed the firm.

The start of the 20th century saw an overwhelming drive for self-improvement, and the stereopticon was found in most parlors. Lloyd Singley saw an even greater potential in this recreational device and expanded his markets to educational programs and promotional lantern slide shows. Keystone View photographers fanned out over the world to create annotated series that taught geography, culture, and art to schoolchildren. At the same time, Singley developed equipment that would be widely used in courses of physical therapy exercise to improve vision. The company became the largest stereo manufacturer in the world, operating from the former Centennial High School building on Market Street. It was bought out by the Mast Company of Iowa, and the thousands of negatives from its vault are now at the University of California, Riverside. A local Keystone View Museum is currently being developed at the former Huidekoper Land Company Office.

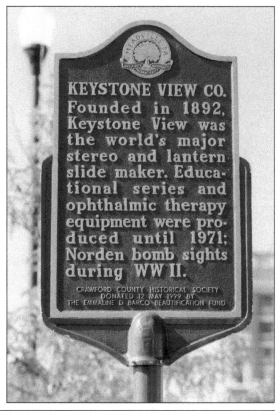

KEYSTONE VIEW CO. Founded in 1892, Keystone View was the world's major stereo and lantern slide maker. Educational series and ophthalmic therapy equipment were produced until 1971; Norden bomb sights during WW II.

CRAWFORD COUNTY HISTORICAL SOCIETY
DONATED 12 MAY 1999 BY
THE EMMALINE D. BARCO BEAUTIFICATION FUND

Keystone View Company,

Meadville, Penna.

One of the first self-propelling agricultural machines manufactured locally was the Minnis steam tractor. Thomas Minnis was a local bookbinder and clerk whose visit to the Great Plains in the mid-19th century had led him to believe that the deep sod of that area would require heavy equipment to break it for farming. While his tractor proved too costly for individual farmer's use, it soon caught on in the lumbering camps of the far Northwest, where it handled steep terrain and mammoth first growth trees with ease.

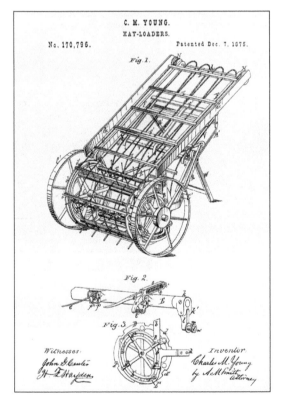

The Meadville area was the center for major dairy production and field crops, and farming improvements were met with general interest and investment. C.M. Young's hay loader was patented in 1875 but looks perfectly familiar to rural populations today.

Born into a farming family at Roundtop, Barrett Foust was well aware of where efficiency could be improved, and his ingenuity provided a number of inexpensive solutions within the reach of small family farms such as thrived in Meadville's surrounding countryside.

In 1929, the farming area around Roundtop, on the left in the scene below, was taken over by a new major industry for Meadville. Attracted by the enormous availability of water and the accessibility of the Erie Railroad mainlines, American Viscose chose Meadville as the location for a major expansion of its rayon production and spinning operations. The plant, as seen in this rendering, was built in 1929, was expanded in 1938, and was a major employer until 1988.

# B. A. Foust Corn Shock Loader

## MEADVILLE, PENNA.

SIMPLE, DURABLE AND CHEAP. CAPACITY 600 POUND
SHOCKS. CAN LOAD A SHOCK EVERY HALF MIN-
UTE. NO LIFTING TO LOAD OR UNLOAD.
EASY TO OPERATE. GOES ON ANY
WAGON AND HAY RACK.

Patented December 26, 1905. December 28, 1908.

## LOADS SHOCKS OF 600 POUNDS

### IS RAPID AND HANDY.

One man in the field with loaders and drivers to keep him busy can load corn faster than any ensilage cutter or husker can possibly use it.

The machine loads any kind of corn, tops of very tall going higher than the track.

It is an advantage to have corn standing when unloading either by hand or with a horse and rope.

A 3-inch eye beam forms the track and is an ideal carrier. Strong and light for the work, weighing less than 100 pounds.

## Self-Measuring Curb Gasoline Station

FILTERED GASOLINE — FILTERED GASOLINE

GASOLINE

These cuts illustrate our Curb Gasoline Station, for measuring and delivering gasoline from underground storage tanks, direct into motor cars, and is for use on the edge of sidewalks.

It is a high grade, long-distance, self-measuring pump, installed within a steel housing case, which locks up when not in use. The pump delivers one full gallon at each full stroke, and has a stop for half gallon, and for quart. It has a "Counter" which records the number of full gallons pumped at a time, up to 15, and returns to zero by pressing a button. We can also, when desired, attach a meter, which records the total number of gallons passing the pump, up to ten thousand, and repeat. Eight feet delivery hose and hose spout is attached to the hose cock, and a faucet provides for drawing into cans or pails. The outfit connects up with underground tank by 1¼ inch pipe, and tank may be located wherever desired.

We can furnish any capacity underground storage tanks, from medium thickness to very heavy, holding from one to twenty barrels, at reasonable prices.

The station is painted red, and lettered as shown, in large aluminum letters, on opposite sides, up and down street. It is 17 inches in diameter, and 66 inches high. Approved by all insurance regulations, as shown on brass plate attached to pump.

Nothing better than this Curb Outfit is made.

Price complete, F. O. B. factory . . . $..........
Gallon meter attached (extra) . . . $..........
Electric light fixture (extra) . . . $..........
Filter (extra) . . . $..........

**BEMAN AUTOMATIC OIL CAN COMPANY, MEADVILLE, PA.**

Beman's Automatic Oil Can had originally been patented as a way to dispense kerosene into containers brought in to general stores by homemakers. Beman then expanded product lines by creating pump systems, which allowed other liquid products such as barrels of molasses and vinegar to be kept in store basements while being dispensed on the first floor. When the automobile arrived on the scene, Beman had the basic patents for systems to dispense gasoline safely from underground storage tanks. The pump shown here is one of the later, more sophisticated models that filtered and measured the gas as it was fed directly into the car's tank.

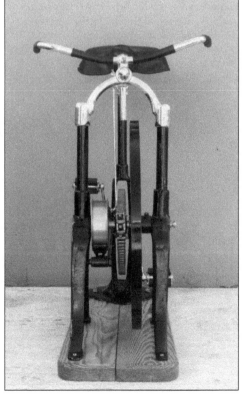

Harry Robinson was a "wheeler," in the slang of the 1890s. Every spare minute available to him was spent on his bicycle, grinding out miles on the county's roads. He was also an entrepreneurial young man, apparently, because he produced, first, an up-to-date atlas of the county's roads; second, a directory of the county's cities, boroughs, townships, villages, crossroads, and post offices; and third, what was apparently the world's first "exercycle." Grounded by long, hard winters, he designed, built, patented, and produced this machine to maintain his wheeling fitness.

The Page Boiler Company was established in the mid-19th century, with its factory in Meadville near the Erie Railroad freight station on South Main Street. A sprawling foundry operation, it produced boilers, steam radiators, and various hot water heaters for home, industrial, and public building use under the trade names Monarch, Volunteer, and Corto. The works were taken over by Talon in its 1930s expansion.

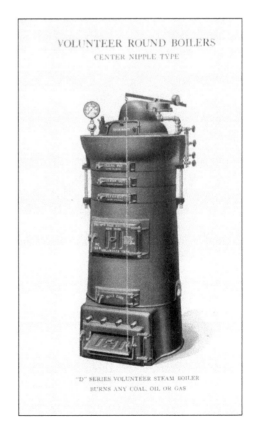

VOLUNTEER ROUND BOILERS
CENTER NIPPLE TYPE

"D" SERIES VOLUNTEER STEAM BOILER
BURNS ANY COAL, OIL OR GAS

Page's products were built to utilize alternative fuels—gas, coal, and oil—and were provided with the latest in safety devices, including thermostats, expansion tanks, and air valves.

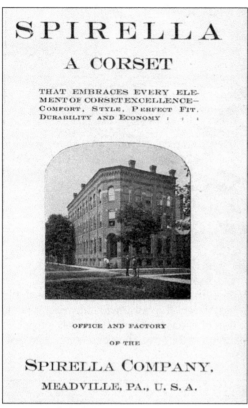

# SPIRELLA

## A CORSET

THAT EMBRACES EVERY ELE-
MENT OF CORSET EXCELLENCE—
COMFORT, STYLE, PERFECT FIT,
DURABILITY AND ECONOMY : : :

OFFICE AND FACTORY

OF THE

## SPIRELLA COMPANY,

MEADVILLE, PA., U. S. A.

This advertising brochure presents the history of the Spirella Corset and a wealth of personal endorsements from obviously respectable satisfied customers. Spirella began in Meadville when M.M. Beeman created a woven, flexible steel stay and engineered the machinery to mass-produce it. His partners were apparently responsible for marketing the corsets through personal fittings by corsetieres in the customer's home, for absolute privacy.

The corset company grew from its modest 1904 two-room start-up to several buildings in Meadville, including the former Chautauquan publishing building (center). By 1920, it had outsold the available work force of the local labor market (more than 700 custom-made corsets a week), and most of its operations moved to Buffalo, New York. Operated on a very paternalistic policy, the company subsidized an employees' association (left), which offered an infirmary, self-improvement clubs and programs, and a library. The company also sponsored a baseball team that competed successfully in the early PONY and Iron Leagues of the period and for whose home games employees were released to attend.

Spirella promotion operated on several levels. These calendar cards, created in the contemporary style of Fisher and Gibson, were apparently mailed on a monthly basis to customers and/or corsetieres in an already international market.

A quite different look was achieved in the corsetiere's catalogue of styles to choose from. The saucy innocence of the female model and the tough-it-out expression of the male are in marked contrast to the determined respectability reflected in the sales brochure or the society image of the calendar.

1914

Working as a corporate lawyer for the Delamater family firm, Col. Lewis Walker traveled extensively. His chance meeting with Whitcomb Judson introduced him to the hookless fastener, and he quickly saw the potential. In 1914, production was begun in this temporary structure on Race Street.

Fifty years later, the hookless fastener had become a Talon zipper, which, although almost universally used, was already feeling the pressure from foreign imports and an arthritic administration. The company had taken over the Meadville Theological School campus when that facility moved away to become part of the University of Chicago. This landmark building was part of an expansion of the school's former refectory building into a production and administrative center. In turn, it has since become a nationally recognized industrial incubator.

The new Gas & Electric system office was built cheek by cheek with the old terminus of the trolley (the major consumer of electricity at that time), at Chestnut and River Streets. The office windows display all the new electric appliances from fans to refrigerators available to make life easier.

Meadville had always been a town of hotels and inns. The Central Hotel was one of the oldest, as the remaining hitching post testifies. This is a puzzle picture. Are those loafers staring at the young woman with the basket or at the camera?—surely no novelty in this *c.* 1910s image.

Henry Utech's drugstore occupied one of the street front retail spaces in the Lafayette Hotel, and this 1929 photograph shows it as fairly typical of the pharmacies of the period. The elaborate mezzanine screen possibly reflects Utech's interest in art, and the small lending library may be another sign of cultural interest in a sea of sundries. Identified are Anthony Nagorski, Henry Utech, and Norman Bender.

Not all sales were confined to store fronts. Here, J Wilson Hamilton with his well-groomed horse and his handsome wagon delivers milk and cream to the door. Typically, he would also provide eggs and other dairy products whose freshness was a matter of concern to the homemaker. The bricked street indicates a post-1900 date.

# Five

# EDUCATION AND RECREATION

Education and recreation went hand in hand in Meadville. Debates (political and otherwise), lectures, musical programs, and theatricals (both home grown and professional circuit performances) absorbed the spare time of Meadville residents.

Allegheny College and the Theological School were the source of countless programs, usually offered free to the community. The churches did their share, bringing in outstanding scholars and exhorters. The Opera House and the Academy of Music offered the programs of professional traveling troupes and served as venues for local productions. Local fire companies and fraternal organizations sponsored bands and orchestras to rival the musicales and recitals of the several music schools.

When a town of less than 20,000 residents supports 2 well-ranked colleges, over 30 churches, 2 business schools, and up to 5 music schools, not to mention 12 regional and national publications ranging from the *Pennsylvania Farmer* to the *Chautauquan*, it is a fair guess that most households will be involved in education or cultural events.

This is not to imply that sports, fairs, and, later, vaudeville and movies, in any way lacked support. Nevertheless, from the day that Jennet Finney opened her dame school on Second Street, education was a recognized priority and self-improvement an automatic goal for the majority of citizens.

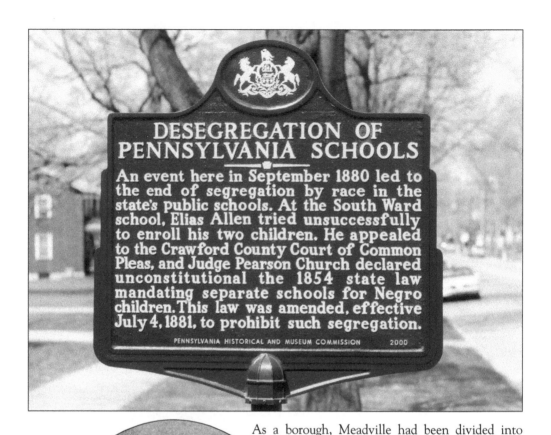

DESEGREGATION OF
PENNSYLVANIA SCHOOLS

An event here in September 1880 led to the end of segregation by race in the state's public schools. At the South Ward school, Elias Allen tried unsuccessfully to enroll his two children. He appealed to the Crawford County Court of Common Pleas, and Judge Pearson Church declared unconstitutional the 1854 state law mandating separate schools for Negro children. This law was amended, effective July 4, 1881, to prohibit such segregation.

PENNSYLVANIA HISTORICAL AND MUSEUM COMMISSION          2000

As a borough, Meadville had been divided into two wards, North Ward and South Ward, each with its separate school board and elementary school. Following the Civil War, the town mushroomed and was incorporated as a city, and the resulting single school board built two new schools, still designated by their former ward names. In 1880, Elias Allen, a black carpenter, tried to register his two young children at the South Ward school nearest their home and was refused under the state education act that mandated separate schools for Negroes when there were more than 20 in a school district. The resulting court decision that the state law was unconstitutional, handed down in 1881 by common pleas Judge Pearson Church, resulted in the desegregation of all the state's schools. Church, who described himself as a Bourbon Democrat, was also the author of a ruling against Standard Oil in the Tidewater pipeline case. He was not reelected to a second term.

189-South Ward School, Meadville Pa

The 1870 building of new schools reflected not only the growth of the city's population but also an increased recognition of the need for better education for the area's children. Leading families donated land for new buildings and donated funds for books and enrichment education programs. The South Ward School (above) was heavily subsidized by the Huidekoper family, and the North Ward School (below) by the Reynolds and Dick families.

206-North Ward School Buildings, Meadville, Pa

Since 1805, the Academy, first at Liberty and Chestnut Streets and then enlarged and rebuilt on Second (Market) Street, had served the secondary schooling needs of the community. As the wider-based elementary schools educated more students to eighth-grade levels, the secondary schools drew higher enrollment and accepted students from surrounding townships. In 1888, the school board built a public high school, Centennial High School, in celebration of Meadville's 100th birthday.

Within a decade, Centennial High School was inadequate to the needs of the new work force for better or higher education, and classes were offered in rented space nearby. By 1925, a new high school, which went on to serve the upper grades and then junior high-level grades for more than 60 years, had been built at the north end of Diamond Park.

Business schools appeared as the city's business, banking, and manufacturing base increased. The Bryant and Stratton chain opened a school, and Miss Boyd's School of Shorthand rapidly developed into the Meadville Commercial College, which offered penmanship, accounting, and business machine training. Located in a downtown business block, it at one point enjoyed an affiliation with Allegheny College.

Founded by Juvia Tinker Hull, the Conservatory of Music reflected the immense degree of interest of area residents in both vocal and instrumental music. This glass plate stereo negative, by Charles Forker, is placed at Chancery Lane and Chestnut Street and is tentatively dated in the early 1890s. By the 1910s, this school had become the Pennsylvania College of Music and was affiliated with Allegheny College. The national sorority Alpha Chi Omega was founded here, and one of the great choral music directors of the 20th century, Morten Luvaas, was director of the school and later professor of music at Allegheny College and director of the nationally known Allegheny Singers. (From the S.D. Clark collection.)

The Meadville Theological School, often referred to as the Unitarian college, was established by Harm Jan Huidekoper as an alternative to the more traditional religious outlook of Allegheny College. First opened in a former church on Center Street near the courthouse, the college was built on the eastern hill of the city just beyond the homes and land office developed by the second and third generation Huidekopers. The buildings were set in a parklike campus. Divinity Hall, located next to the library, was the classroom building for the upper Chestnut Street campus, shown in this 1906 postcard.

The Class of 1861 is identified by last names only, from left to right, Fox, Moose, Higgen, Barber, Chapin, Thayer, Brown, Green, and Black.

130    Hunnywell Hall, Unitarian College, Meadville, Pa.

Hunneywell Hall, a 20th-century addition to the Meadville Theological School campus, provided dining, recreation, and social space for the student body. When the school was incorporated into the University of Chicago in the 1920s, the burgeoning Hookless Fastener-Talon Inc. acquired the campus and utilized this building as its corporate headquarters, building massive manufacturing space behind and to the east along Pine Street to consolidate its growing operations.

An important aspect of the Unitarian college's mission was its ecumenical outreach, and it brought lecturers and visitors from around the world to its campus. Posing on the porch at Sunnyside, the president's home in 1900 are, from left to right, the Reverend Henry Barber, Bifrim Chandra Pae, and the Reverend Earl Wilbur.

Although members of the extended Huidekoper family were all actively involved in support of the Meadville Theological School, Harm Jan's unmarried daughter, Aunt Lizzie, carried much of the organizational load. At one point (following the death of her brother Frederick) she served as chairperson of the board of the school. Her 1854 home, at the corner of Chestnut and Grove Streets, was a center to which the family, faculty, and students gravitated. The girl posing at the corner in this 1907 picture is not identified, but carefully noted is the young Bald Cypress tree, another of the specimen trees so cherished by Meadville residents.

The south facade of Allegheny College's Bentley Hall looks out across the city. The view here is across the Ravine and Rustic Bridge from North Main Street. For many years, the bridge was the key for official entry into coed status, sealed by a date's kiss.

Class reunions became an integral part of Allegheny's tradition, as this 35th reunion photograph of the Class of 1880 indicates. Pictured, from left to right, are Gilbert A. Nodine, attorney; Anna B. Carter (Mrs. L.L. Davis); Frank Lippitt, businessman; Charles A. Ensign, druggist; Frank Solomon Chryst, attorney; George S. Miner, missionary; Ida M. Tarbell; journalist; and Arthur L. Bates, congressman. Today, the names of Tarbell, as author of the Standard Oil history, and Bates, as the proponent of the Pearl Harbor Naval Station, are immediately recognizable. Why a sign to "Keep Back of Bentley" was deemed necessary is unknown but may relate somehow to the fact that the Class of 1881 had once managed to steal 1880s granite boulder.

In 1879, Marcus Hulings of Oil City donated funds to build a Ladies Hall and thereby recognized the permanence of the addition of females to the student body. In a paper read at that year's commencement, Ida Tarbell said "we were allowed to come to Allegheny College, and shall remain . . . each one of us has a heart-felt gratitude that this hall has been begun . . ." Referring to the women who would be educated at Allegheny, she went on "They will have a foundation so firm that their womanhood will not yield, They will become so strong and self-reliant that they will be able to benefit and not hinder the world."

Successive administrations have made substantial additions to the campus. South Hall, later designated Shultz Hall, was added as a women's dorm, dining hall, infirmary, and admissions office in the 1960s.

In the early years of Allegheny College, the library was housed in Bentley and then in Ruter Halls. As part of the centennial expansion of the college, under Pres. William H. Crawford, a new and separate library building was built to house the college's outstanding collection, dating back to the first gifts in 1815.

In recognition of a quarter of a century of outstanding service to Allegheny, a new library and learning center was named for retiring president Dr. Lawrence L. Pelletier in 1974.

Nineteenth-century gas balloons were not as colorful as today's hot-air balloons, but they had the same power to capture the imagination and the hearts of the public. The Thurstons routinely made ascensions for celebrations, and the four sequential images shown here were taken at a July 4, 1891 ascension at Diamond Park in front of the Crawford House hotel. Having filled the envelope, Alic Thurston and a passenger cast off the ballast sandbags and prepare to fly heading southeast in a slight breeze. As the balloon rises, a small gust pushes it into the overhead wire of the streetlight.

The impact of the wire spills a substantial amount of gas and tips from the basket Thurston, who fortunately has a strong hold on the landing line. The balloon continues east up Chestnut Street with Thurston just visible pulling himself back into the basket. The flight continued at low altitude until the aeronauts found a clearing for landing. The amazing thing is that Thurston continued to fly from city venues for another 20 years.

In this view from the south end of Diamond Park looking west, the 1876 Centennial Celebration Committee poses for a deserved tribute to their evergreen arches topped by Pennsylvania's seal.

The view from the west, looking up Chestnut Street, shows the arch displaying Liberty, with busts of three presidents—Abraham Lincoln, George Washington, and perhaps Andrew Jackson, a local favorite.

The War of 1812 had had a major impact on the local area, with a militia encampment of 3,000 at Meadville assigned to intercept the expected British invasion from Canada. These veterans of 1812–1813 gathered in 1876 at the Cullum House for their third reunion, belying the belief that men of the period did not often reach old age.

The Cullum House, seen at the east end of the Dock Street (Mead Avenue) bridge in this early stereo image by Charles Forker, was managed by S.W. Kepler, whose father, Jacob Kepler, had served three enlistments in 1812. The Forker image also provides an excellent view of the Atlantic & Great Western station and its McHenry Hotel. The Mead Avenue Bridge, now on the Historic American Engineering Register, was only six years old when this view was taken. (The S.D. Clark collection.)

The delivery of armament and gunpowder to Commodore Perry at Lake Erie was reenacted *c.* 1913, as seen in this view taken as the caravan passed through Kerrtown on the old Mercer Pike, accompanied by early cars and the inevitable small boys.

Patriotic themes invariably brought good response from the public, and the touring Liberty Bell was no exception. This scene, taken in 1893, was repeated at every railroad siding in the county.

114

When the Opera House, a second-floor theater, burned *c.* 1880, the move to replace it with a full-scale, self-contained theater building was immediate. J.M. Wood, a theater architect of national reputation, was hired to design the structure and, by 1885, it was ready to welcome the touring theatrical troupes of the period. Below, *Lucia di Lammermoor* is presented.

Programs ranged from Otis Skinner and other such uplifting lecturers to tragedy and light opera to minstrel and early vaudeville, including Mrs. Tom Thumb who, following her husband's death, continued to travel with a variety show that included Japanese acrobats.

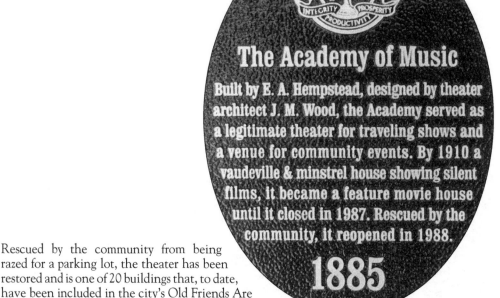

MEADVILLE·PA
INTEGRITY PROSPERITY
PRODUCTIVITY

**The Academy of Music**

Built by E. A. Hempstead, designed by theater architect J. M. Wood, the Academy served as a legitimate theater for traveling shows and a venue for community events. By 1910 a vaudeville & minstrel house showing silent films, it became a feature movie house until it closed in 1987. Rescued by the community, it reopened in 1988.

**1885**

Rescued by the community from being razed for a parking lot, the theater has been restored and is one of 20 buildings that, to date, have been included in the city's Old Friends Are Worth Keeping program.

A late-19th- and early-20th-century characteristic of Meadville was music. Every volunteer and civic group appears to have had some musical organization attached and, for marching bands, often a very elaborate uniform. Shown is Hope Hose Company, mustered on Market Square *c.* 1880s with its horse-drawn equipment.

The temperance movement is well represented on the musical scene. Membership in these groups seems to have been exclusively male.

Major employers obviously thought it worth their while to invest in subsidizing bands, as this 1917 picture indicates. There is substantial evidence that these groups performed not only at hometown parades and celebrations but made excursions to some distance to take part in community celebrations.

Following World War I, veterans organizations continued the tradition of military music. This undated photograph shows the American Legion Stafford Post on the steps of Meadville High School.

These Civil War soldiers are apparently engaged in spontaneous and informal music making since it seems unlikely that any stringed instrument was part of their military baggage. There is no identification of the military organization.

A small brass ensemble accompanies the German Rifle Corps on Arch Street. Whether this view dates from before, during, or after the Civil War is unknown.

The term "orchestra" seems a bit ambitious applied to eight men, but the Northwestern Orchestra was a prestigious late-19th-century group, apparently a winter activity for the Northwestern Band.

The tradition of a community orchestra continued up to World War II, as this 1938 photo documents. The orchestra is seen on the stage of Meadville High School and includes among its members a few women.

Clearly with all the musical activity in Meadville, music stores prospered. This view of the Edward T. Bates Company documents the addition of seven pianos to its inventory. It is also an interesting view of the transition of horse-drawn to automotive cartage *c.* 1915.

Dancing Pavilion, Oakwood Park,
Meadville, Pa.

Oakwood Park as a trolley destination had several heavily promoted attractions, one of which was the dance pavilion with its spring floor. The extensive veranda area allowed for cooling strolls between sets. The park was the site of the first "flickers" shown in Meadville and of the daring jumps by a bloomer-clad woman parachutist from Alic Thurston's tethered gas balloon.

The Meadville Mutuals were national champions in 1875, but there is no record of the team members' names.

By 1912, Allegheny was fielding teams in most sports. Few of the pictures identify individual names. This picture of an eight-man squad was taken on the steps of the college's new Montgomery Gymnasium.

Heavily padded suits and tight leather helmets characterized the protective clothing of high school football players in 1909. Meadville High School attendance was augmented by tuition students from surrounding townships. The school generally fielded a large squad and was considered a sports power in the county. This view was taken at the Spirella field, Athletic Park.

Sports minded young men could go on to play with essentially semipro teams by choosing their place of work. The Erie Railroad and Spirella teams were among the most noted ones. In 1953, Meadville Master Antenna brought the television signal clearly into Meadville, and sports became a passive pleasure.

RESCUE SQUAD
Elmer Miller
Emil Solomon
Frank Gillespie

*Tribune Newspapers Go Through*

**HIGH WATERS DIDN'T STOP** Tribune Newspaper carrier boys from getting Tuesday's Evening Republican to customers. Here Carrier Peter SEVERO of Poplar Street, braves flood waters in hip boots to deliver.

About 100 papers also were delivered to Fifth Ward. Where water was too deep for boots, Tribune Circulation Manager Calvin Kost and members of Meadville Rescue Squad transported carrier boys in boats. —Tribune Photo by Mitchell

In the late 19th and into the 20th century, Meadville was the frequent victim of flooding by French Creek. Until the 1959 flood, which made national television, the estimated cost of flood control was deemed too high and scenes like this 1951 front-page photograph were not uncommon. It would seem that Calvin Kost, at the oars, as circulation manager, found this a better idea than newsboy Peter Severo who, weighed down by a bag of papers, has a white-knuckle grip on the boat. Rescue squad members Elmer Miller (left) and Emil Solomon seem to be taking it all in stride.

Bird's-eye views of communities were predecessors of today's aerial views and often gave a remarkably accurate picture of an area's development. This 1870 view emphasizes the Atlantic & Great Western rail yards, station, hotel, and workers' housing on the island. It

also shows the old main branch of French Creek still filled with water. All clearly placed at Allegheny College's campus (upper left) are Bentley, Hulings, and Ruter Halls and the Culver boarding hall.

# ACKNOWLEDGMENTS

This book would not have been possible without the very generous cooperation of the Crawford County Historical Society (CCHS) and its archivist Laura Polo, who allowed unfettered access to the photographic files. Thanks also to Ben Cares Photographic Arts; to William Owens, photographer; to Jed Miller, without whose assistance the images could not have been transmitted; and to Bill Moore, who so kindly read copy and suggested better approaches. Special thanks are due generations of Meadville residents who have preserved the images of the past and have given them into the care of the CCHS Archives. May their tribe increase.

Ingram Content Group UK Ltd.
Milton Keynes UK
UKHW031356070323
418135UK00004B/107